AUGUSTA READ THOMAS

RUMI SETTINGS

FOR VIOLIN AND VIOLONCELLO

Rumi Settings was commissioned by
the Arizona Friends of Chamber Music and:
Marya and Robert Giesy, Henry Weiss for Marion Hersh,
Carla Rosenlicht in memory of Maxwell Rosenlicht, Mr. and Mrs.
Charles M. Peters, Jean-Paul Bierny and Chris Tanz.

The first performance took place on 5 March, 2002 in Tucson, Arizona
by Ani Kavafian, violin and Ida Kavafian, viola.

duration ca. 9 minutes

ED 4364
First Printing: April 2010

ISBN: 978-1-4234-3027-8

G. SCHIRMER, *Inc.*

Composer's Note:

My favorite moment in any piece of music is the moment of maximum risk and striving. Whether the venture is tiny or large, loud or soft, fragile or strong, passionate, erratic, ordinary or eccentric...! Maybe another way to say this is the moment of exquisite humanity and raw soul. All art that I cherish has an element of love and recklessness and desperation. I like music that is alive and jumps off the page and out of the instrument as if **something big is at stake.**

When I read this beautiful poem by Rumi, written 800 years ago, all of it but especially the last 3 lines resonated deeply inside of me. I felt deeply compelled to set it as a song without words, trying to capture its intensely personal, fiery, honest meaning.

I was thrilled and honored to receive a commission from the Arizona Friends of Chamber Music which provided me a much cherished and fantastic opportunity to compose *Rumi Settings* which Ani and Ida Kavafian premiered in March 2002 in Tucson.

The work has a total duration of 9 minutes and is made up of 4 short movements that can be played attacca or with short pauses between them.

Each of the movements adheres to the meaning, perfume, and essence of the stunning Rumi text. Throughout the score, each line of the text is written above the music, corresponding to the moment when the duo is depicting that particular line of the poem, thus the musicians know the connotation and nuance of the composition.

It would take far too long to describe each line of text and their corresponding musical adventures. So allow me to modestly offer six brief examples of this procedure.

The music starts with a passionate, dramatic, cadenza-like surge in the violin, played with the whole soul engaged and as *"if it does not matter if the instrument breaks"* (not literally) until the cello soon enters, supporting and propelling the music forward onto a kaleidoscopic journey. A climax ensues before the music relaxes and *"We have fallen into the place where everything is music"* settling on a calm open fifth.

In Movement II you will hear notes *"rising into the atmosphere"* as the two soloists arpeggiate ascending chords with double stops. Suddenly, *"the whole world's harp"* rushes forward in full motion with pizzicati until later the movement ends, in a distant, still calm, such that we can discern, *"there will still be hidden instruments playing."*

Movement III is extremely graceful and tuneful, like *"a pearl from the ocean floor..."*

Rumi Settings is dedicated with admiration and gratitude to Ani and Ida Kavafian and the Arizona Friends of Chamber Music.

—Augusta Read Thomas

Performance Notes:

Grace notes come before the beat.

All pizzicati are to be played *l.v. molto.*

String bowing suggestions and preferences are marked by the composer but can be altered at the discretion of the players.

Throughout movement III, most of the sustained "Ds" are suggested to be played as harmonics.

The four movements of this piece may be played attacca or with short pauses between them. The composer prefers attacca.

WHERE EVERYTHING IS MUSIC

Rumi (ca. 1240)

[Movement I]

Don't worry about saving these songs!
And if one of our instruments breaks,
it doesn't matter.

We have fallen into the place
where everything is music.

[Movement II]

The strumming and the flute notes
rise into the atmosphere,
and even if the whole world's harp
should burn up, there will still be
hidden instruments playing.

So the candle flickers and goes out.
We have a piece of flint, and a spark.

[Movement III]

This singing art is sea foam.
The graceful movements come from a pearl
somewhere on the ocean floor.

Poems reach up like spindrift and the edge
of driftwood along the beach, wanting!

They derive
from a slow and powerful root
that we can't see.

[Movement IV]

Stop the words now.
Open the window in the center of your chest,
and let the spirits fly in and out.

—Coleman Barks, translator

"Where Everything is Music" from "The Essential Rumi"
is used by permission of Coleman Barks

dedicated with admiration and gratitude to Ani and Ida Kavafian and the Arizona Friends of Chamber Music

RUMI SETTINGS

I

Augusta Read Thomas
(2001)

Copyright © 2002, 2010 by G. Schirmer, Inc. (ASCAP), New York, NY
International Copyright Secured. All Rights Reserved.
Warning: Unauthorized reproduction of this publication is prohibited by Federal law and subject to criminal prosecution.

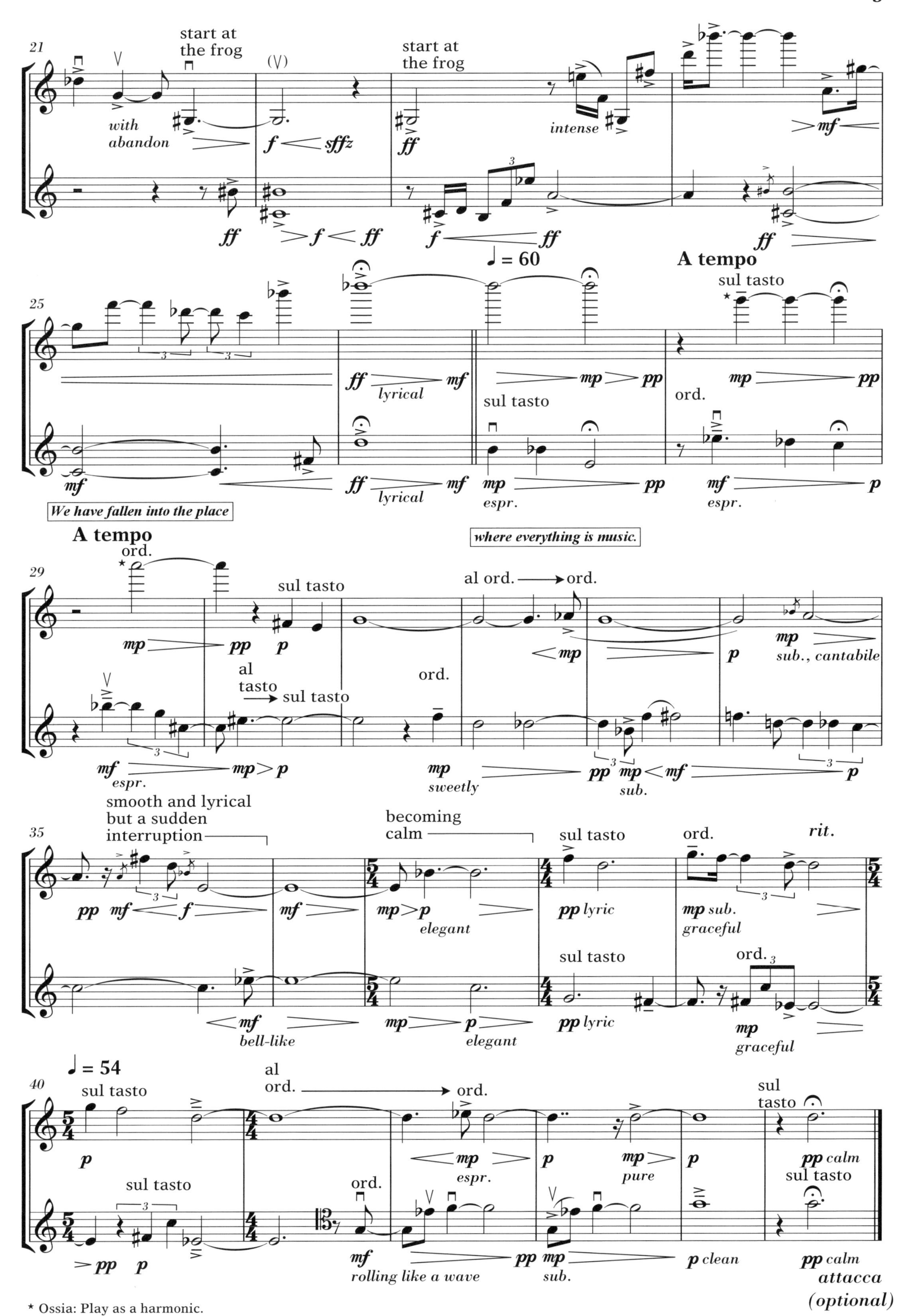

* Ossia: Play as a harmonic.

II

* Trill slow to fast.

AUGUSTA READ THOMAS

RUMI SETTINGS

FOR VIOLIN AND VIOLONCELLO

Rumi Settings was commissioned by
the Arizona Friends of Chamber Music and:
Marya and Robert Giesy, Henry Weiss for Marion Hersh,
Carla Rosenlicht in memory of Maxwell Rosenlicht, Mr. and Mrs.
Charles M. Peters, Jean-Paul Bierny and Chris Tanz.

The first performance took place on 5 March, 2002 in Tucson, Arizona
by Ani Kavafian, violin and Ida Kavafian, viola.

duration ca. 9 minutes

ED 4364
First Printing: April 2010

ISBN: 978-1-4234-3027-8

G. SCHIRMER, *Inc.*

Composer's Note:

My favorite moment in any piece of music is the moment of maximum risk and striving. Whether the venture is tiny or large, loud or soft, fragile or strong, passionate, erratic, ordinary or eccentric...! Maybe another way to say this is the moment of exquisite humanity and raw soul. All art that I cherish has an element of love and recklessness and desperation. I like music that is alive and jumps off the page and out of the instrument as if **something big is at stake.**

When I read this beautiful poem by Rumi, written 800 years ago, all of it but especially the last 3 lines resonated deeply inside of me. I felt deeply compelled to set it as a song without words, trying to capture its intensely personal, fiery, honest meaning.

I was thrilled and honored to receive a commission from the Arizona Friends of Chamber Music which provided me a much cherished and fantastic opportunity to compose *Rumi Settings* which Ani and Ida Kavafian premiered in March 2002 in Tucson.

The work has a total duration of 9 minutes and is made up of 4 short movements that can be played attacca or with short pauses between them.

Each of the movements adheres to the meaning, perfume, and essence of the stunning Rumi text. Throughout the score, each line of the text is written above the music, corresponding to the moment when the duo is depicting that particular line of the poem, thus the musicians know the connotation and nuance of the composition.

It would take far too long to describe each line of text and their corresponding musical adventures. So allow me to modestly offer six brief examples of this procedure.

The music starts with a passionate, dramatic, cadenza-like surge in the violin, played with the whole soul engaged and as *"if it does not matter if the instrument breaks"* (not literally) until the cello soon enters, supporting and propelling the music forward onto a kaleidoscopic journey. A climax ensues before the music relaxes and "*We have fallen into the place where everything is music*" settling on a calm open fifth.

In Movement II you will hear notes *"rising into the atmosphere"* as the two soloists arpeggiate ascending chords with double stops. Suddenly, "*the whole world's harp*" rushes forward in full motion with pizzicati until later the movement ends, in a distant, still calm, such that we can discern, "*there will still be hidden instruments playing.*"

Movement III is extremely graceful and tuneful, like "*a pearl from the ocean floor...*"

Rumi Settings is dedicated with admiration and gratitude to Ani and Ida Kavafian and the Arizona Friends of Chamber Music.

—Augusta Read Thomas

Performance Notes:

Grace notes come before the beat.

All pizzicati are to be played *l.v. molto.*

String bowing suggestions and preferences are marked by the composer but can be altered at the discretion of the players.

Throughout movement III, most of the sustained "Ds" are suggested to be played as harmonics.

The four movements of this piece may be played attacca or with short pauses between them. The composer prefers attacca.

WHERE EVERYTHING IS MUSIC

Rumi (ca. 1240)

[Movement I]

Don't worry about saving these songs!
And if one of our instruments breaks,
it doesn't matter.

We have fallen into the place
where everything is music.

[Movement II]

The strumming and the flute notes
rise into the atmosphere,
and even if the whole world's harp
should burn up, there will still be
hidden instruments playing.

So the candle flickers and goes out.
We have a piece of flint, and a spark.

[Movement III]

This singing art is sea foam.
The graceful movements come from a pearl
somewhere on the ocean floor.

Poems reach up like spindrift and the edge
of driftwood along the beach, wanting!

They derive
from a slow and powerful root
that we can't see.

[Movement IV]

Stop the words now.
Open the window in the center of your chest,
and let the spirits fly in and out.

—Coleman Barks, translator

"Where Everything is Music" from "The Essential Rumi"
is used by permission of Coleman Barks

dedicated with admiration and gratitude to Ani and Ida Kavafian and the Arizona Friends of Chamber Music

RUMI SETTINGS

I

Don't worry about saving these songs! And if one of our instruments breaks, it doesn't matter.

Augusta Read Thomas
(2001)

Copyright © 2002, 2010 by G. Schirmer, Inc. (ASCAP), New York, NY
International Copyright Secured. All Rights Reserved.
Warning: Unauthorized reproduction of this publication is prohibited by Federal law and subject to criminal prosecution.

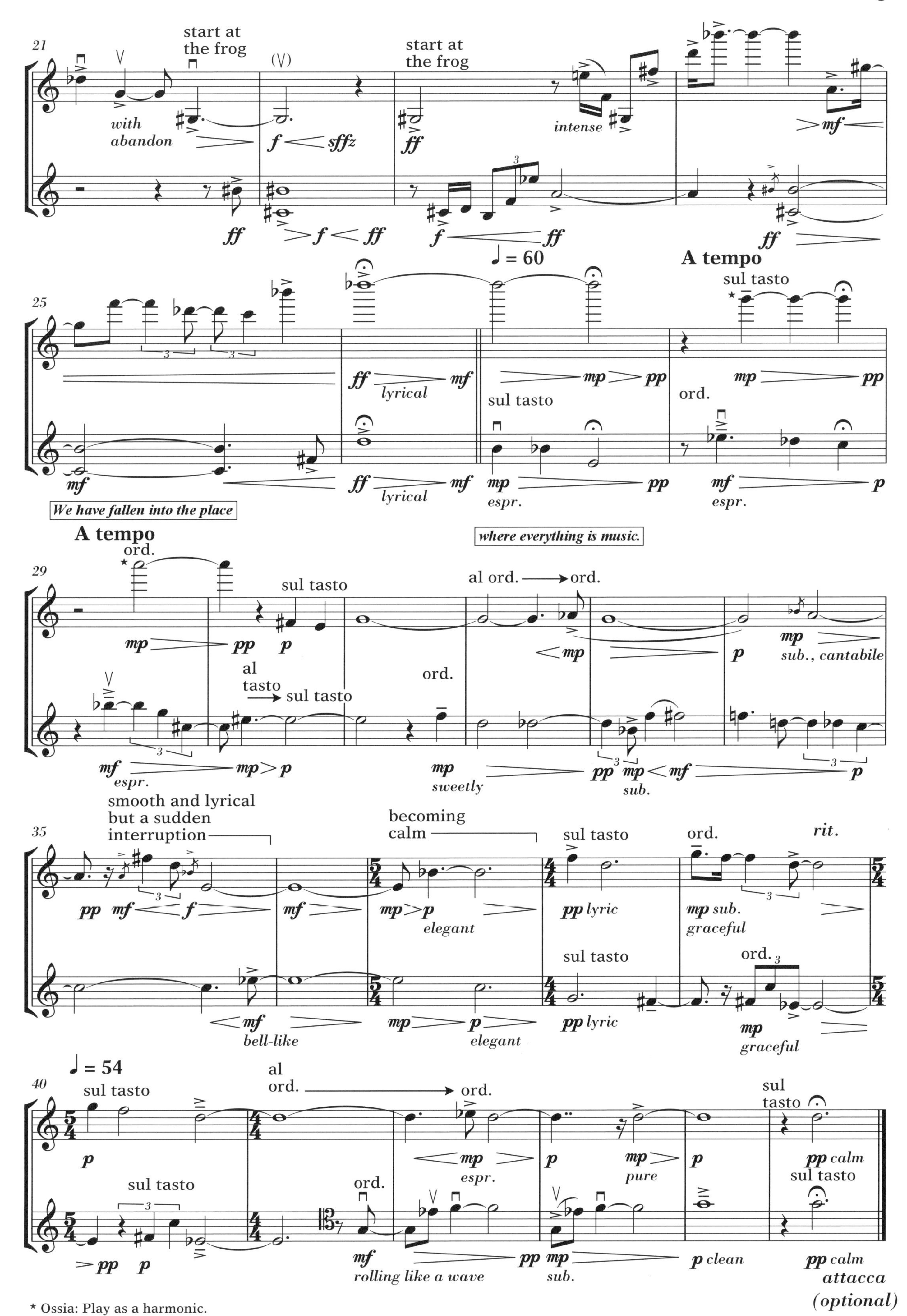

* Ossia: Play as a harmonic.

II

* Trill slow to fast.

* Trill slow to fast.

III

This singing art is sea foam.
The graceful movements come from a pearl somewhere in the ocean floor.
Suspended and graceful
♩ = 52
molto rubato sempre
(ord.)
mf sempre
with dynamic nuance
(ord.)
p
mp sempre
elegant
f sempre, with dynamic nuance
mp subito e sempre
molto rubato sempre
f sempre, lyrical,
with dynamic nuance
f subito
e sempre
pp
mp
sub.
pp
sub.
mp
f sempre
espr.

Poems reach up like spindrift and the edge of driftwood along the beach, wanting!
14
f
bell-like
ff
ff bell-like
mf
mp sempre
mp sempre
elegant
18
f sempre
21
f sub.
p
mp
mp sub.
f sub.
24
f sub.
mp sub.
mp sub.
f sub.
They derive from a slow and powerful root that we can't see.
27
f sub.
ff
mf
sffz
mp sub.
f
ff
mf
sffz
attacca
(optional)

IV

Passionate ♩ = 63
Stop
the
words
now.
ff
f
sffz
ff intense
ff dramatic
pp sub.
elegant
f
ff
p
sffz
♪ = ♪ sempre
mp espr.
ffp
pp
sub.
p
mp
pp
cantabile
sffz
ff
athletic and intense
ffp
ff sempre
dramatic
sub.
ff espr.

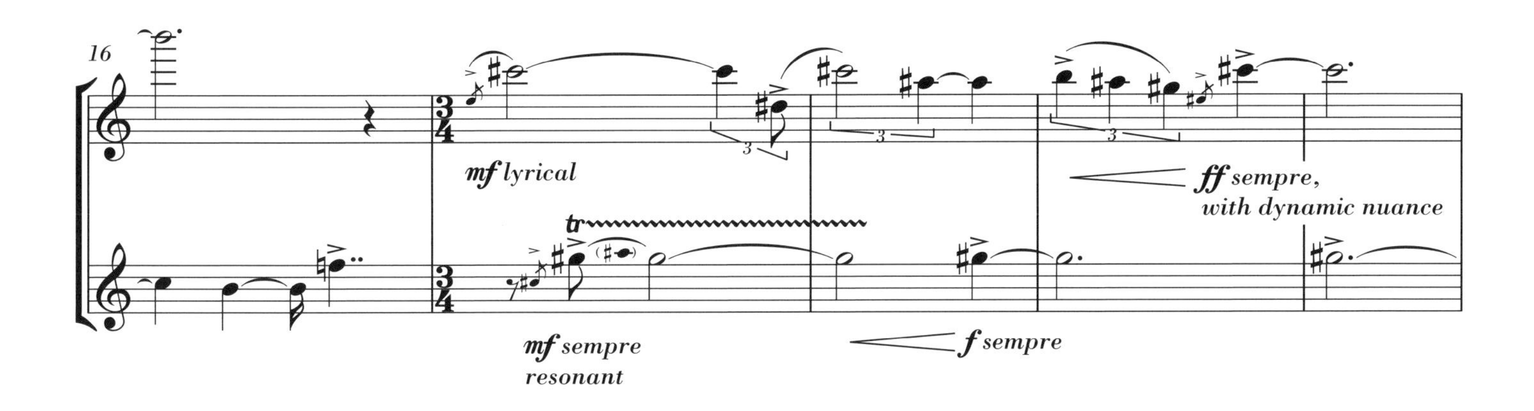
16
mf lyrical
ff sempre,
with dynamic nuance
tr
mf sempre
resonant
f sempre

21
stately
ff sempre

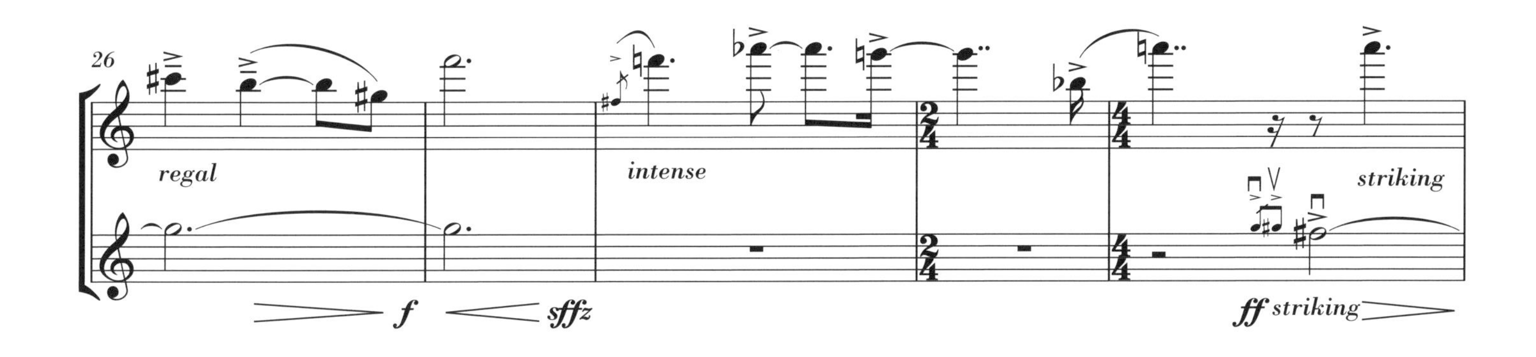
26
regal
intense
striking
f
sffz
ff striking

Open the window in the center of your chest and let the spirits fly in and out.
31
molto rubato
non dim.
f
ff sempre
non dim.

* Trill slow to fast.

III

This singing art is sea foam.
The graceful movements come from a pearl somewhere in the ocean floor.
Suspended and graceful
♩ = 52
molto rubato sempre
(ord.)
mf sempre
with dynamic nuance
(ord.)
p
mp sempre
elegant
f sempre, with dynamic nuance
mp subito e sempre
molto rubato sempre
f sempre, lyrical,
with dynamic nuance
f subito
e sempre
pp
sub.
mp
pp
sub.
mp
f sempre
espr.

Poems reach up like spindrift and the edge of driftwood along the beach, wanting!
f
bell-like
ff
mp sempre
ff bell-like
mf
mp sempre
elegant
f sempre
f sub.
mp sub.
p
mp
f sub.
f sub.
mp sub.
mp sub.
f sub.
They derive from a slow and powerful root that we can't see.
f sub.
ff
mf
sffz
mp sub.
f
ff
mf
sffz
attacca
(optional)

IV

Passionate ♩ = 63
Stop
the
words
now.
ff
f
sffz
ff intense
ff dramatic
pp sub.
elegant
ff
p
sffz
mp espr.
ffp
pp
sub.
♪ = ♪ sempre
mp
p
pp
cantabile
sffz
ff
ff
athletic and intense
ffp
ff sempre
dramatic
p
sub.
ff espr.

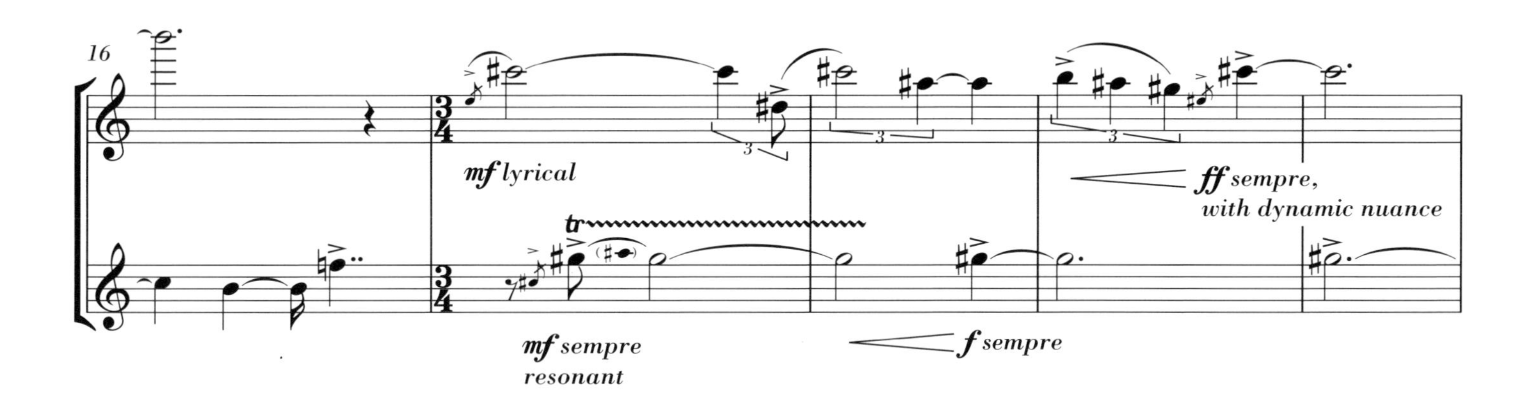
16
mf lyrical
ff sempre,
with dynamic nuance
mf sempre
resonant
f sempre

21
stately
ff sempre

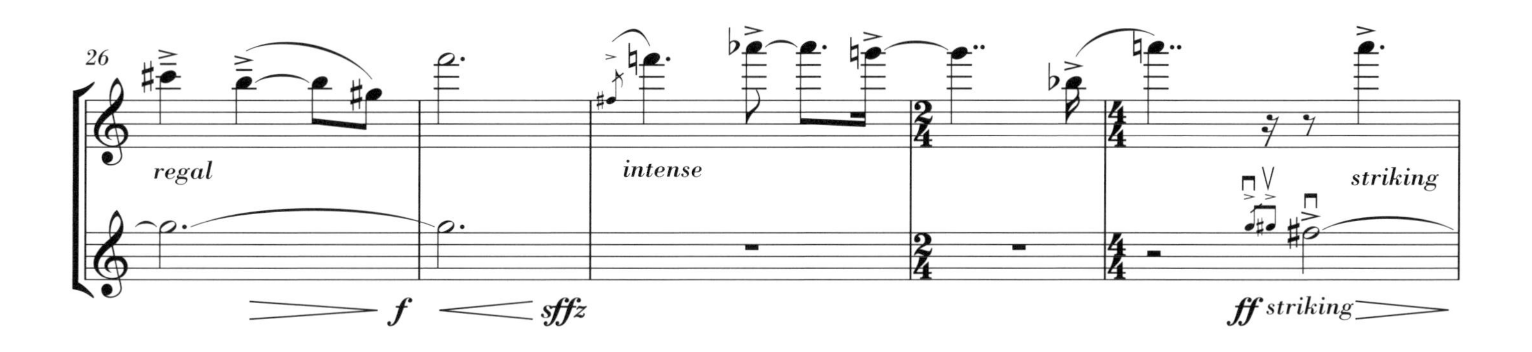
26
regal
intense
striking
f
sffz
ff striking

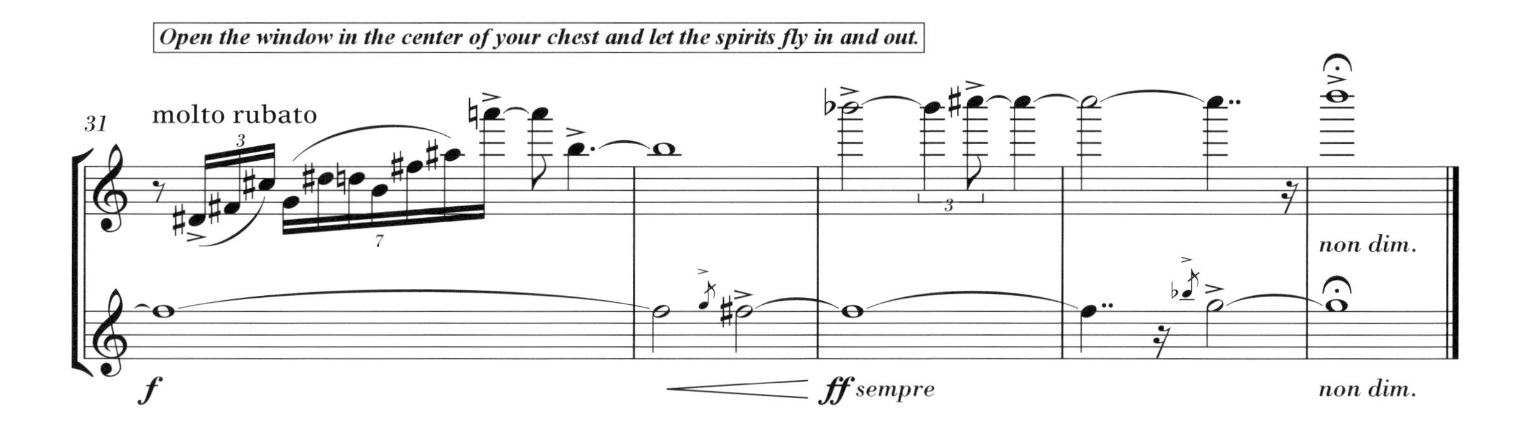
Open the window in the center of your chest and let the spirits fly in and out.
31
molto rubato
non dim.
f
ff sempre
non dim.